Simply Air Fryer

Cookbook 2021

The Essential Guide To Cooking Affordable, Easy
and Delicious Air Fryer Crisp Recipes for
Everyone

Lisa Cameron

Disclaimer Notice:

Please note the information contained within this document is for educational and entertainment purposes only. All effort has been executed to present accurate, up to date, and reliable, complete information. No warranties of any kind are declared or implied. Readers acknowledge that the author is not engaging in the rendering of legal, financial, medical or professional advice. The content within this book has been derived from various sources. Please consult a licensed professional before attempting any techniques outlined in this book.

By reading this document, the reader agrees that under no circumstances is the author responsible for any losses, direct or indirect, which are incurred as a result of the use of information contained within this document, including, but not limited to, — errors, omissions, or inaccuracies

Table Of Content

Introduction

Congratulations on purchasing your copy of **Simply Air Fryer Cookbook 2021: The Essential Guide To Cooking Affordable, Easy and Delicious Air Fryer Crisp Recipes for Everyone**, and thank you for doing so.

I'm glad you chose to take this opportunity to welcome the air fryer diet into your life. I'm sure this book will help you find all the information and tools you need to better integrate the Air Fryer Diet plan with your habits.

In addition, I thought I'd share with you some delicious ideas and recipes for all tastes and the best of your low carb diet that I hope you'll enjoy.

You'll find hundreds of easy-to-make ideas that will best suit your situation or needs of the moment, with all the preparation times, portion sizes and a list of all the nutritional values you'll need.

BREAKFAST

Veggie Frittata

Preparation Time: 17 minutes

Servings: 4

Ingredients:

- 6 large eggs.

- ¼ cup chopped yellow onion.

- ¼ cup chopped green bell pepper.

- ½ cup chopped broccoli.

- ¼ cup heavy whipping cream.

Directions:

1. Take a large bowl, whisk eggs and heavy whipping cream. Mix in broccoli, onion and bell pepper.

2. Pour into a 6-inch round oven-safe baking dish. Place baking dish into the air fryer basket. Adjust the temperature to 350 Degrees F and set the timer for 12 minutes

3. Eggs should be firm and cooked fully when the frittata is done. Serve warm.

Nutrition: Calories: 168; Protein: 10.2g; Fiber: 0.6g; Fat: 11.8g; Carbs: 3.1g

Avocado Cauliflower Toast

Preparation Time: 23 minutes

Servings: 2

Ingredients:

- 1, 12-oz.steamer bag cauliflower

- ½ cup shredded mozzarella cheese

- 1 large egg.

- 1 ripe medium avocado

- ½ tsp. garlic powder.

- ¼ tsp. ground black pepper

Directions:

1. Cook cauliflower according to package instructions. Remove from bag and place into cheesecloth or clean towel to remove excess moisture.

2. Place cauliflower into a large bowl and mix in egg and mozzarella. Cut a piece of parchment to fit your air fryer basket

3. Separate the cauliflower mixture into two and place it on the parchment in two mounds. Press out the cauliflower

mounds into a ¼-inch-thick rectangle. Place the parchment into the air fryer basket.

4. Adjust the temperature to 400 Degrees F and set the timer for 8 minutes

5. Flip the cauliflower halfway through the cooking time

6. When the timer beeps, remove the parchment and allow the cauliflower to cool 5 minutes.

7. Cut open the avocado and remove the pit. Scoop out the inside, place it in a medium bowl and mash it with garlic powder and pepper. Spread onto the cauliflower.

Nutrition: Calories: 278; Protein: 14.1g; Fiber: 8.2g; Fat: 15.6g; Carbs: 15.9g

Breakfast Zucchini

Preparation Time: 5 minutes

Cooking time: 35 minutes

Servings: 4

Ingredients:

- 4 zucchinis, diced into 1-inch pieces, drained

- 2 small bell pepper, chopped medium

- 2 small onion, chopped medium

- Cooking oil spray

- Pinch salt and black pepper

Directions:

1. Preheat the Air fryer to 350 o F and grease the Air fryer basket with cooking spray.

2. Season the zucchini with salt and black pepper and place in the Air fryer basket.

3. Select Roasting mode and cook for about 20 minutes, stirring occasionally.

4. Add onion and bell pepper and cook for 5 more minutes.

5. Remove from the Air fryer and mix well to serve warm.

Nutrition:

Calories: 146, Fat: 0.5g, Carbohydrates: 3.8g, Sugar: 5.5g, Protein: 4g, Sodium: 203mg

Tuna and Spring Onions Salad

Preparation Time: 20 minutes

Servings: 4

Ingredients:

- 14 oz. canned tuna, drained and flaked

- 2 spring onions; chopped.

- 1 cup arugula

- 1 tbsp. olive oil

- A pinch of salt and black pepper

Directions:

1. In a bowl, all the ingredients except the oil and the arugula and whisk.

2. Preheat the Air Fryer over 360°F, add the oil and grease it. Pour the tuna mix, stir well and cook for 15 minutes

3. In a salad bowl, combine the arugula with the tuna mix, toss and serve.

Nutrition: Calories: 212; Fat: 8g; Fiber: 3g; Carbs: 5g; Protein: 8g

Mushroom and Tomato Frittata

Preparation Time: 15 minutes

Cooking time: 14 minutes

Servings: 2

Ingredients:

- 1 bacon slice, chopped

- 6 cherry tomatoes, halved

- 6 fresh mushrooms, sliced

- 3 eggs

- ½ cup Parmesan cheese, grated

- 1 tablespoon olive oil

- Salt and black pepper, to taste

Directions:

1. Preheat the Air fryer to 390 o F and grease a baking dish lightly.

2. Mix together bacon, mushrooms, tomatoes, salt and black pepper in the baking dish.

3. Arrange the baking dish into the Air Fryer basket and cook for about 6 minutes.

4. Whisk together eggs in a small bowl and add cheese.

5. Mix well and pour over the bacon mixture.

6. Place the baking dish in the Air Fryer basket and cook for about 8 minutes.

7. Dish out and serve hot.

Nutrition:

Calories: 397, Fat: 26.2g, Carbohydrates: 23.3g, Sugar: 11.2g, Protein: 27.3g, Sodium: 693mg

Red Cabbage Bowls

Preparation Time: 20 minutes

Servings: 4

Ingredients:

- 2 cups red cabbage; shredded

- 1 red bell pepper; sliced

- 1 small avocado, peeled, pitted and sliced

- A drizzle of olive oil

- Salt and black pepper to taste.

Directions:

1. Grease your air fryer with the oil, add all the ingredients, toss, cover and cook at 400°F for 15 minutes.

2. Divide into bowls and serve cold for breakfast

Nutrition: Calories: 209; Fat: 8g; Fiber: 2g; Carbs: 4g; Protein: 9g

MAIN

Potato and Carrot with Vegan Cheese

Preparation time: 10 minutes • Cooking time: 16 minutes • Servings: 6

INGREDIENTS

- 2potatoes, cubed
- 3pounds carrots, cubed
- 1yellow onion, chopped
- Salt and black pepper to the taste
- 1teaspoon thyme, dried
- 3tablespoons coconut milk
- 2teaspoons curry powder
- 3tablespoons vegan cheese, crumbled
- 1tablespoon parsley, chopped

DIRECTIONS

1. In your air fryer's pan, mix onion with potatoes, carrots, salt, pepper, thyme and curry powder, stir, cover and cook at 365 degrees F for 16 minutes.
2. Add coconut milk, sprinkle vegan cheese, divide between plates and serve.
3. Enjoy!

NUTRITION: Calories 241, Fat 4, Fiber 7, Carbs 8, Protein 4

Simple Quinoa Stew

Preparation time: 10 minutes Cooking time: 15 minutes
Servings: 6

INGREDIENTS

- ½ cup quinoa
- 30ounces canned black beans, drained
- 28ounces canned tomatoes, chopped
- 1green bell pepper, chopped
- 1yellow onion, chopped
- 2sweet potatoes, cubed
- 1tablespoon chili powder
- 2tablespoons cocoa powder
- 2teaspoons cumin, ground
- Salt and black pepper to the taste
- ¼ teaspoon smoked paprika

DIRECTIONS

1. In your air fryer, mix quinoa, black beans, tomatoes, bell pepper, onion, sweet potatoes, chili powder, cocoa, cumin, paprika, salt and pepper, stir, cover and cook on High for 6 hours.
2. Divide into bowls and serve hot.
3. Enjoy!

NUTRITION: Calories 342, Fat 6, Fiber 7, Carbs 18, Protein 4

Mexican Casserole

Preparation time: 10 minutes • Cooking time: 15 minutes •
Servings: 4

INGREDIENTS

- 1tablespoon olive oil
- 4garlic cloves, minced
- 1yellow onion, chopped
- 2tablespoons cilantro, chopped
- 1small red chili, chopped
- 2teaspoons cumin, ground
- Salt and black pepper to the taste
- 1teaspoon sweet paprika
- 1teaspoon coriander seeds
- 1pound sweet potatoes, cubed
- Juice of ½ lime
- 10ounces green beans
- 2cups tomatoes, chopped
- 1tablespoon parsley, chopped

DIRECTIONS

1. Grease a pan that fits your air fryer with the oil,
   add garlic, onion, cilantro, red chili, cumin, salt,
   pepper, paprika, coriander, potatoes, lime juice,
   green beans and tomatoes, toss, place in your air
   fryer and cook at 365 degrees F for 15 minutes.

2. Add parsley, divide between plates and serve.

3. Enjoy!

NUTRITION: Calories 223, Fat 5, Fiber 4, Carbs 7, Protein 8

Green Beans with Carrot

Preparation time: 10 minutes Cooking time: 12 minutes

Servings: 4

INGREDIENTS

- 1pound green beans
- 1yellow onion, chopped
- 4carrots, chopped
- 4garlic cloves, minced
- 1tablespoon thyme, chopped
- 3tablespoons tomato paste
- Salt and black pepper to the taste

DIRECTIONS

1. In your air fryer's pan, mix green beans with onion, carrots, garlic, tomato paste,, salt and pepper, stir, cover and cook at 365 degrees F for 12 minutes.
2. Add thyme, stir, divide between plates and serve.
3. Enjoy!

NUTRITION: Calories 231, Fat 4, Fiber 6, Carbs 7, Protein 5

Cauliflower Stew with Tomatoes and Green Chilies

Scallions and Endives with Rice

Preparation time: 10 minutes • Cooking time: 20 minutes • Servings: 4

INGREDIENTS

- 1tablespoon olive oil
- 2scallions, chopped
- 3garlic cloves chopped
- 1tablespoon ginger, grated
- 1teaspoon chili sauce
- A pinch of salt and black pepper
- ½ cup white rice
- 1cup veggie stock
- 3endives, trimmed and chopped

DIRECTIONS

1. Grease a pan that fits your air fryer with the oil, add scallions, garlic, ginger, chili sauce, salt, pepper, rice, stock and endives, place in your air fryer, cover and cook at 365 degrees F for 20 minutes.
2. Divide casserole between plates and serve.
3. Enjoy!

NUTRITION: Calories 220, Fat 5, Fiber 8, Carbs 12, Protein 6

Cabbage and Tomatoes

Preparation time: 10 minutes • Cooking time: 12 minutes • Servings: 4

INGREDIENTS

- 1tablespoon olive oil
- 1green cabbage head, chopped
- Salt and black pepper to the taste
- 15ounces canned tomatoes, chopped
- ½ cup yellow onion, chopped
- 2teaspoons turmeric powder

DIRECTIONS

4. In a pan that fits your air fryer, combine oil with green cabbage, salt, pepper, tomatoes, onion and turmeric, place in your air fryer and cook at 365 degrees F for 12 minutes.
5. Divide between plates and serve.
6. Enjoy!

NUTRITION: Calories 202, Fat 5, Fiber 8, Carbs 9, Protein 10

Eggplant Stew

Preparation time: 10 minutes • Cooking time: 15 minutes • Servings: 4

INGREDIENTS

- 24ounces canned tomatoes, chopped
- 1red onion, chopped
- 2red bell peppers, chopped
- 2big eggplants, roughly chopped
- 1tablespoon smoked paprika
- 2teaspoons cumin, ground
- Salt and black pepper to the taste
- Juice of 1 lemon
- 1tablespoons parsley, chopped

DIRECTIONS

1. In your air fryer's pan, mix tomatoes with onion, bell peppers, eggplant, smoked paprika, cumin, salt, pepper and lemon juice, stir, cover and cook at 365 degrees F for 15 minutes
2. Add parsley, stir, divide between plates and serve cold.
3. Corn, Mushrooms and Cabbage Salad Enjoy!

NUTRITION: Calories 251, Fat 4, Fiber 6, Carbs 14, Protein 3

Okra and Corn Mix

Preparation time: 10 minutes • Cooking time: 15 minutes •
Servings: 6

INGREDIENTS

- 1green bell pepper, chopped
- 1small yellow onion, chopped
- 3garlic cloves, minced
- 16ounces okra, sliced
- 2cup corn
- 12ounces canned tomatoes, crushed
- 1and ½ teaspoon smoked paprika
- 1teaspoon marjoram, dried
- 1teaspoon thyme, dried
- 1teaspoon oregano, dried
- Salt and black pepper to the taste

DIRECTIONS

1. In your air fryer, mix bell pepper with onion, garlic, okra, corn, tomatoes, smoked paprika, marjoram, thyme,

   oregano, salt and pepper, stir, cover and cook at 360 degrees F for 15 minutes.
2. Stir, divide between plates and serve.
3. Enjoy!

NUTRITION: Calories 243, Fat 4, Fiber 6, Carbs 10, Protein 3

SIDES

Cinnamon Pumpkin

Wedges

Preparation Time: 15 minutes

Cooking time: 8 minutes

Servings: 2

Ingredients:

- 1 teaspoon raisins

- 12 oz pumpkin

- 1 teaspoon ground cinnamon

- 1 teaspoon butter

- 5 tablespoon water

- 2 tablespoon brown sugar

- 1 teaspoon fresh ginger, grated

Directions:

1. Peel the pumpkin and cut it into the serving wedges.

2. Melt the butter and combine it together with the ground cinnamon, brown sugar, and grated ginger.

3. Churn the mixture gently.

4. Rub every pumpkin wedge with the butter mixture well. Leave it.

5. Preheat the air fryer to 390 F.

6. Pour water into the air fryer basket.

7. Add raisins and pumpkin wedges.

8. After this, add all the remaining juice from the pumpkin wedges.

9. Cook the pumpkin for 5 minutes.

10. After this, flip the pumpkin wedges into another side.

11. Cook the pumpkin wedges for 3 minutes more.

12. Then transfer the cooked pumpkin wedges into the serving plates.

13. Sprinkle the pumpkin wedges with the raisins.

14. Enjoy!

Nutrition: calories 119, fat 2.5, fiber 5.7, carbs 25.4, protein 2.1

Roasted Cauliflower Head

Preparation Time: 10 minutes

Cooking time: 17 minutes

Servings: 2

Ingredients:

- 12 oz cauliflower head

- 2 tablespoon cream

- 1 tablespoon flour

- ½ teaspoon ground black pepper

- 1 teaspoon turmeric

- 1 teaspoon salt - 1 teaspoon olive oil

Directions:

1. Wash the cauliflower head carefully.

2. Combine the cream and flour in the bowl.

3. Add ground black pepper and turmeric.

4. Whisk the mixture.

5. Then sprinkle the cauliflower head with the cream mixture. Let the cauliflower soaks the cream.

6. Sprinkle the cauliflower with salt.

7. Preheat the air fryer to 360 F.

8. Put the cauliflower r head in the air fryer tray.

9. Cook the vegetables for 12 minutes.

10. After this, sprinkle the cauliflower with the olive oil.

11. Cook the cauliflower head for 5 minutes at 390 F.

12. When the cauliflower is cooked – it will have the light brown crusted surface.

13. Serve it and enjoy!

Nutrition: calories 90, fat 3.3, fiber 4.7, carbs 13.4, protein 4

Tomato Endives Mix

Preparation time: 5 minutes

Cooking time: 10 minutes

Servings: 4

Ingredients:

- 8 endives, trimmed

- Juice of 1 lime

- 1 tablespoon tomato sauce

- 2 tablespoons cilantro, chopped

- 1 teaspoon sugar

- Salt and black pepper to taste

- 3 tablespoons avocado oil

Directions:

1. In a bowl, mix all of the ingredients well, then transfer to your air fryer's basket.

2. Cook at 370 degrees F for 10 minutes.

3. Divide between plates and serve as a side dish.

Nutrition: calories 199, fat 6, fiber 6, carbs 9, protein 6

Stuffed Portobello Mushrooms

Preparation Time: 15 minutes

Cooking time: 6 minutes

Servings: 2

Ingredients:

- 2 Portobello mushroom hats

- 2 slices Cheddar cheese

- ¼ cup panko breadcrumbs

- ½ teaspoon salt

- ½ teaspoon ground black pepper

- 1 egg

- 1 teaspoon oatmeal

- 2 oz bacon, chopped cooked

Directions:

1. Crack the egg into the bowl and whisk it.

2. Combine the ground black pepper, oatmeal, salt, and breadcrumbs in the separate bowl.

3. Dip the mushroom hats in the whisked egg.

4. After this, coat the mushroom hats in the breadcrumb mixture.

5. Preheat the air fryer to 400 F.

6. Place the mushrooms in the air fryer basket tray and cook for 3 minutes.

7. After this, put the chopped bacon and sliced cheese over the mushroom hats and cook the meal for 3 minutes.

8. When the meal is cooked – let it chill gently.

9. Enjoy!

Nutrition: calories 376, fat 24.1, fiber 1.8, carbs 14.6, protein 25.2

Creamy Spinach

Preparation Time: 15 minutes

Cooking time: 10 minutes

Servings: 2

Ingredients:

- ¼ cup cream

- 1 tablespoon cream cheese

- 1 cup spinach

- ½ onion, diced, boiled

- ½ teaspoon salt

- 1 teaspoon butter

- ½ teaspoon ground black pepper

- 2 bacon slices, cooked, chopped

- ½ teaspoon paprika

Directions:

1. Preheat the air fryer to 330 F.

2. Toss the butter in the air fryer basket and melt.

3. Meanwhile, chop the spinach and sprinkle it with the salt.

4. Let the spinach gives the juice.

5. When the butter is melted – put the spinach with the remaining juice in the air fryer basket.

6. Sprinkle the spinach with the cream cheese, cream, diced onion, ground black pepper, and paprika.

7. Stir the mixture gently with the help of the wooden spatula.

8. Cook the spinach for 5 minutes.

9. After this, stir the spinach gently and add chopped bacon.

10. Cook the spinach for 5 minutes more.

11. Then stir the cooked meal carefully.

12. Transfer the cooked spinach to the serving plates.

13. Serve it!

Nutrition: calories 174, fat 13.4, fiber 1.3, carbs 5.1, protein 8.6

SEAFOOD

Tuna Steaks with Pearl Onions

Preparation Time: 20 minutes

Servings: 4

Nutrition: 332 Calories; 5.9g Fat; 10.5g Carbs; 56.1g Protein; 6.1g Sugars

Ingredients

- 4 tuna steaks

- 1 pound pearl onions

- 4 teaspoons olive oil

- 1 teaspoon dried rosemary

- 1 teaspoon dried marjoram

- 1 tablespoon cayenne pepper

- 1/2 teaspoon sea salt

- 1/2 teaspoon black pepper, preferably freshly cracked

- 1 lemon, sliced

Directions

1. Place the tuna steaks in the lightly greased cooking basket. Top with the pearl onions; add the olive oil, rosemary, marjoram, cayenne pepper, salt, and black pepper.

2. Bake in the preheated Air Fryer at 400 degrees F for 9 to 10 minutes. Work in two batches.

3. Serve warm with lemon slices and enjoy!

Cajun Fish Cakes with Cheese

Preparation Time: 30 minutes

Servings: 4

Nutrition: 478 Calories; 30.1g Fat; 27.2g Carbs; 23.8g Protein; 2g Sugars

Ingredients

- 2 catfish fillets

- 1 cup all-purpose flour

- 3 ounces butter

- 1 teaspoon baking powder

- 1 teaspoon baking soda

- 1/2 cup buttermilk

- 1 teaspoon Cajun seasoning

- 1 cup Swiss cheese, shredded

Directions

1. Bring a pot of salted water to a boil. Boil the fish fillets for 5 minutes or until it is opaque. Flake the fish into small pieces.

2. Mix the remaining ingredients in a bowl; add the fish and mix until well combined. Shape the fish mixture into 12 patties.

3. Cook in the preheated Air Fryer at 380 degrees F for 15 minutes. Work in batches. Enjoy!

English-Style Flounder Fillets

Preparation Time: 20 minutes

Servings: 2

Nutrition: 432 Calories; 16.7g Fat; 29g Carbs; 38.4g Protein; 2.7g Sugars

Ingredients

- 2 flounder fillets

- 1/4 cup all-purpose flour

- 1 egg

- 1/2 teaspoon Worcestershire sauce

- 1/2 cup bread crumbs

- 1/2 teaspoon lemon pepper

- 1/2 teaspoon coarse sea salt

- 1/4 teaspoon chili powder

Directions

1. Rinse and pat dry the flounder fillets.

2. Place the flour in a large pan.

3. Whisk the egg and Worcestershire sauce in a shallow bowl. In a separate bowl, mix the bread crumbs with the lemon pepper, salt, and chili powder.

4. Dredge the fillets in the flour, shaking off the excess. Then, dip them into the egg mixture. Lastly, coat the fish fillets with the breadcrumb mixture until they are coated on all sides.

5. Spritz with cooking spray and transfer to the Air Fryer basket. Cook at 390 degrees for 7 minutes.

6. Turn them over, spritz with cooking spray on the other side, and cook another 5 minutes. Bon appétit!

Smoked Halibut and Eggs in Brioche

Preparation Time: 25 minutes

Servings: 4

Nutrition: 372 Calories; 13.1g Fat; 22g Carbs; 38.6g Protein; 3.3g Sugars

Ingredients

- 4 brioche rolls

- 1 pound smoked halibut, chopped

- 4 eggs

- 1 teaspoon dried thyme

- 1 teaspoon dried basil

- Salt and black pepper, to taste

Directions

1. Cut off the top of each brioche; then, scoop out the insides to make the shells.

2. Lay the prepared brioche shells in the lightly greased cooking basket.

3. Spritz with cooking oil; add the halibut. Crack an egg into each brioche shell; sprinkle with thyme, basil, salt, and black pepper.

4. Bake in the preheated Air Fryer at 325 degrees F for 20 minutes. Bon appétit!

Spicy Cod

Preparation Time: 10 minutes

Cooking time: 11 minutes

Servings: 2

Ingredients:

- 2, 6-ounces>-1½-inch thickcod fillets

- 1 teaspoon smoked paprika

- 1 teaspoon cayenne pepper

- 1 teaspoon onion powder

- 1 teaspoon garlic powder

- Salt and ground black pepper, as required

- 2 teaspoons olive oil

Directions:

1. Preheat the Air fryer to 390 o F and grease an Air fryer basket.

2. Drizzle the salmon fillets with olive oil and rub with the all the spices.

3. Arrange the salmon fillets into the Air fryer basket and cook for about 11 minutes.

4. Dish out the salmon fillets in the serving plates and serve hot.

Nutrition:

Calories: 277, Fat: 15.4g, Carbohydrates: 2.5g, Sugar: 0.9g, Protein: 33.5g, Sodium: 154mg

Korean-Style Salmon Patties

Preparation Time: 15 minutes

Servings: 4

Nutrition: 396 Calories; 20.1g Fat; 16.7g Carbs; 35.2g Protein; 3.1g Sugars

Ingredients

- 1 pound salmon

- 1 egg

- 1 garlic clove, minced

- 2 green onions, minced

- 1/2 cup rolled oats

Sauce:

- 1 teaspoon rice wine

- 1 ½ tablespoons soy sauce

- 1 teaspoon honey

- A pinch of salt

- 1 teaspoon gochugaru, Korean red chili pepper flakes

Directions

1. Start by preheating your Air Fryer to 380 degrees F. Spritz the Air Fryer basket with

cooking oil.

2. Mix the salmon, egg, garlic, green onions, and rolled oats in a bowl; knead with your hands until everything is well incorporated.

3. Shape the mixture into equally sized patties. Transfer your patties to the Air Fryer basket.

4. Cook the fish patties for 10 minutes, turning them over halfway through.

5. Meanwhile, make the sauce by whisking all ingredients. Serve the warm fish patties with the sauce on the side.

POULTRY

Quick and Easy Chicken Mole

Preparation Time: 35 minutes

Servings: 4

Nutrition: 453 Calories; 17.5g Fat; 25.1g Carbs;

47.5g Protein; 12.9g Sugars

Ingredients

- 8 chicken thighs, skinless, bone-in

- 1 tablespoon peanut oil

- Sea salt and ground black pepper, to taste

Mole sauce:

- 1 tablespoon peanut oil

- 1 onion, chopped

- 1 ounce dried negro chiles, stemmed, seeded, and chopped

- 2 garlic cloves, peeled and halved

- 2 large-sized fresh tomatoes, pureed

- 2 tablespoons raisins

- 1 ½ ounces bittersweet chocolate, chopped

- 1 teaspoon dried Mexican oregano

- 1/2 teaspoon ground cumin

- 1 teaspoon coriander seeds

- A pinch of ground cloves

- 4 strips orange peel

- 1/4 cup almonds, sliced and toasted

Directions

1. Start by preheating your Air Fryer to 380 degrees F. Toss the chicken thighs with the peanut oil, salt, and black pepper.

2. Cook in the preheated Air Fryer for 12 minutes; flip them and cook an additional 10 minutes; reserve.

3. To make the sauce, heat 1 tablespoon of peanut oil in a saucepan over medium-high heat. Now, sauté the onion, chiles and garlic until fragrant or about 2 minutes.

4. Next, stir in the tomatoes, raisins, chocolate, oregano, cumin, coriander seeds, and cloves. Let it simmer until the sauce has slightly thickened.

5. Add the reserved chicken to the baking pan; add the sauce and cook in the preheated Air Fryer at 360 degrees F for

10 minutes or until thoroughly warmed.

7. Serve garnished with orange peel and sliced almonds. Enjoy!

Spiced Chicken Breasts

Servings: 4

Preparation Time: 20 minutes

Cooking Time: 23 minutes

Ingredients

- 2 tablespoons butter, melted

- ¼ teaspoon garlic powder

- ¼ teaspoon onion powder

- ¼ teaspoon smoked paprika

- Salt and ground black pepper, as required

- 4, 6-ouncesboneless, skinless chicken breasts

Instructions

1. In a bowl, mix together butter, and spices.

2. Coat the chicken breasts evenly with the butter mixture.

3. Set the temperature of Air Fryer to 350 degrees F. Grease an Air Fryer basket.

4. Arrange chicken breasts into the prepared Air Fryer basket in a single layer.

5. Air Fry for about 15 minutes.

6. Flip the chicken breasts and Air Fry for 5-8 more minutes.

7. Remove from Air Fryer and transfer the chicken breasts onto a serving platter.

8. Serve hot.

Nutrition:

Calories: 376

Carbohydrate: 0.3g

Protein: 49.3g

Fat: 18.4g

Sugar: 0.1g

Sodium: 226mg

>-**Note: We can avoid the chicken breasts from touching each other by placing the chicken pieces against the sides of air fryer basket.**

Oats Crusted Chicken Breasts

Servings: 2

Preparation Time: 20 minutes

Cooking Time: 12 minutes

Ingredients

- 2, 6-ounceschicken breasts

- Salt and ground black pepper, as required

- ¾ cup oats

- 2 tablespoons mustard powder

- 1 tablespoon fresh parsley

- 2 medium eggs

Instructions

1. Put the chicken breasts onto a cutting board and with a meat mallet, flatten each into even thickness.

2. Then, cut each breast in half.

3. Sprinkle the chicken pieces with salt and black pepper and set aside.

4. In a blender, add the oats, mustard powder, parsley, salt and black pepper. Pulse until a coarse breadcrumb like mixture is formed.

5. Transfer the oat mixture into a shallow bowl.

6. In another bowl, crack the eggs and beat well.

7. Coat the chicken with oats mixture and then, dip into beaten eggs and again, coat with the oats mixture.

8. Set the temperature of Air Fryer to 350 °F. Grease a grill pan of Air Fryer.

9. Arrange chicken breasts into the prepared grill pan in a single layer.

10. Air Fry for about 12 minutes, flipping once halfway through.

11. Remove from Air Fryer and transfer the chicken breasts onto a serving platter.

12. Serve hot.

Nutrition:

Calories: 556

Carbohydrate: 25.1g

Protein: 61.6g

Fat: 22.2g

Sugar: 1.4g

Sodium: 289mg

Crispy Chicken Tenders

Servings: 3

Preparation Time: 20 minutes

Cooking Time: 30 minutes

Ingredients

- 2, 6-ouncesboneless, skinless chicken breasts, pounded into ½-inch thickness and cut into tenders

- ¾ cup buttermilk

- 1½ teaspoons Worcestershire sauce, divided

- ½ teaspoon smoked paprika, divided

- Salt and ground black pepper, as required

- ½ cup all-purpose flour

- 1½ cups panko breadcrumbs

- ¼ cup Parmesan cheese, finely grated

- 2 tablespoons butter, melted

- 2 large eggs

Instructions

1. In a large bowl, mix together buttermilk, ¾ teaspoon of Worcestershire sauce, ¼ teaspoon of paprika, salt, and black pepper.

2. Add in the chicken tenders and refrigerate overnight.

3. In another bowl, mix together the flour, remaining paprika, salt, and black pepper.

4. Place the remaining Worcestershire sauce and eggs in a third bowl and beat until well combined.

5. Mix well the panko, Parmesan, and butter in a fourth bowl.

6. Remove the chicken tenders from bowl and discard the buttermilk.

7. Coat the chicken tenders with flour mixture, then dip into egg mixture and finally coat with the panko mixture.

8. Set the temperature of air fryer to 400 degrees F. Grease an air fryer basket.

9. Arrange chicken tenders into the prepared air fryer basket in 2 batches in a single layer.

10. Air fry for about 13-15 minutes, flipping once halfway through.

11. Remove from air fryer and transfer the chicken tenders onto a serving platter.

12. Serve hot.

Nutrition

Calories: 654

Carbohydrate: 28g

Protein: 454g

Fat: 25.5g

Sugar: 3.9g

Sodium: 399mg

Adobo Seasoned Chicken with Veggies

Preparation Time: 1 hour 30 minutes

Servings: 4

Nutrition: 427 Calories; 15.3g Fat; 18.5g Carbs; 52.3g Protein; 9.4g Sugars

Ingredients

- 2 pounds chicken wings, rinsed and patted dry

- 1 teaspoon coarse sea salt

- 1/4 teaspoon ground black pepper

- 1/2 teaspoon red pepper flakes, crushed

- 1 teaspoon ground cumin

- 1 teaspoon paprika

- 1 teaspoon granulated onion

- 1 teaspoon ground turmeric

- 2 tablespoons tomato powder

- 1 tablespoon dry Madeira wine

- 2 stalks celery, diced

- 2 cloves garlic, peeled but not chopped

- 1 large Spanish onion, diced

- 2 bell peppers, seeded and sliced

- 4 carrots, trimmed and halved

- 2 tablespoons olive oil

Directions

1. Toss all ingredients in a large bowl. Cover and let it sit for 1 hour in your refrigerator.

2. Add the chicken wings to a baking pan.

3. Roast the chicken wings in the preheated Air Fryer at 380 degrees F for 7 minutes.

4. Add the vegetables and cook an additional 15 minutes, shaking the basket once or twice. Serve warm.

Simple Chicken Wings

Servings: 2

Preparation Time: 10 minutes

Cooking Time: 25 minutes

Ingredients

- 1 pound chicken wings

- Salt and ground black pepper, as required

Instructions

1. Set the temperature of Air Fryer to 380 degrees F. Generously, grease an Air Fryer basket.

2. Sprinkle the chicken wings evenly with salt and black pepper.

3. Arrange chicken wings into the prepared Air Fryer basket in a single layer.

4. Air Fry for about 25 minutes, flip the wings once halfway through.

5. Remove from Air Fryer and transfer the chicken wings onto a serving platter.

6. Serve hot.

Nutrition

Calories: 431 Carbohydrate: 0g Protein: 65.6g

Fat: 16.8g Sugar: 0g Sodium: 273mg

Cheesy Chicken Breasts

Servings: 2

Preparation Time: 20 minutes

Cooking Time: 22 minutes

Ingredients

- 2, 6-ounceschicken breasts

- 1 egg, beaten

- 4 ounces' breadcrumbs

- 1 tablespoon fresh basil

- 2 tablespoons vegetable oil

- ¼ cup pasta sauce

- ¼ cup Parmesan cheese, grated

Instructions

1. In a shallow bowl, beat the egg.

2. In another bowl, add the oil, breadcrumbs, and basil and mix until a crumbly mixture forms.

3. Now, dip each chicken breast into the beaten egg and then, coat with the breadcrumb mixture.

4. Set the temperature of Air Fryer to 350 degrees F. Grease an Air Fryer basket.

5. Arrange chicken breasts into the prepared basket

6. Air Fry for about 15 minutes.

7. Spoon the pasta sauce evenly over chicken breast and sprinkle with cheese.

8. Air Fry for about 5-7 more minutes.

9. Remove from Air Fryer and transfer the chicken breasts onto a serving platter.

10. Serve hot.

Nutrition

Calories: 623

Carbohydrate: 44.3g

Protein: 51g

Fat: 25.8g

Sugar: 6.2g

Sodium: 739mg

Spice Lime Chicken

Tenders

Preparation Time: 20 minutes

Servings: 6

Nutrition: 422 Calories; 29.2g Fat; 6.1g Carbs; 32.9g Protein; 2.4g Sugars

Ingredients

- 1 lime

- 2 pounds chicken tenderloins cut up

- 1 cup cornflakes, crushed

- 1/2 cup Parmesan cheese, grated

- 1 tablespoon olive oil

- Sea salt and ground black pepper, to taste

- 1 teaspoon cayenne pepper

- 1/3 teaspoon ground cumin

- 1 teaspoon chili powder

- 1 egg

Directions

1. Squeeze the lime juice all over the chicken.

2. Spritz the cooking basket with a nonstick cooking spray.

3. In a mixing bowl, thoroughly combine the cornflakes, Parmesan, olive oil, salt, black pepper, cayenne pepper, cumin, and chili powder.

4. In another shallow bowl, whisk the egg until well beaten. Dip the chicken tenders in the egg, then in cornflakes mixture.

5. Transfer the breaded chicken to the prepared cooking basket. Cook in the preheated Air Fryer at 380 degrees F for 12 minutes. Turn them over halfway through the cooking time. Work in batches. Serve immediately.

MEAT

Coconut and Chili Pork

Preparation Time: 30 minutes

Servings: 4

Ingredients:

- 4 pork chops

- 2 garlic cloves; minced

- 1 shallot; chopped

- 1 ½ cups coconut milk

- 3 tbsp. coconut aminos

- 2 tbsp. olive oil

- 2 tsp. chili paste

- Salt and black pepper to taste.

Directions:

1. In a pan that fits your air fryer, mix the pork the rest of the ingredients, toss, introduce the pan in the fryer and cook at 400°F for 25 minutes, shaking the fryer halfway.

2. Divide everything into bowls and serve.

Nutrition: Calories: 267; Fat: 12g; Fiber: 4g; Carbs: 6g; Protein: 18g

Beef and Broccoli Stir-Fry

Preparation Time: 1 hour 20 minutes

Servings: 2

Ingredients:

- ½ lb. sirloin steak, thinly sliced

- 2 tbsp. soy sauce, or liquid aminos

- ¼ tsp. grated ginger

- ¼ tsp. finely minced garlic

- 1 tbsp. coconut oil

- 2 cups broccoli florets

- ¼ tsp. crushed red pepper

- ⅛ tsp. xanthan gum

- ½ tsp. sesame seeds

Directions:

1. To marinate beef, place it into a large bowl or storage bag and add soy sauce, ginger, garlic and coconut oil. Allow to marinate for 1 hour in refrigerator.

2. Remove beef from marinade, reserving marinade and place beef into the air fryer basket. Adjust the temperature to 320 Degrees F and set the timer for 20 minutes

3. After 10 minutes, add broccoli and sprinkle red pepper into the fryer basket and shake.

4. Pour the marinade into a skillet over medium heat and bring to a boil, then reduce to simmer. Stir in xanthan gum and allow to thicken

5. When air fryer timer beeps, quickly empty fryer basket into skillet and toss. Sprinkle with sesame seeds. Serve immediately.

Nutrition: Calories: 342; Protein: 27.0g; Fiber: 2.7g; Fat: 18.9g; Carbs: 9.6g

Lamb Chops and Mint Sauce

Preparation Time: 29 minutes

Servings: 4

Ingredients:

- 8 lamb chops

- 1 cup mint; chopped

- 1 garlic clove; minced

- 2 tbsp. olive oil

- Juice of 1 lemon

- A pinch of salt and black pepper

Directions:

1. In a blender, combine all the ingredients except the lamb and pulse well.

2. Rub lamb chops with the mint sauce, put them in your air fryer's basket and cook at 400°F for 12 minutes on each side

3. Divide everything between plates and serve.

Nutrition: Calories: 284; Fat: 14g; Fiber: 3g; Carbs: 6g; Protein: 16g

Moroccan Lamb

Preparation Time: 35 minutes Servings: 4

Ingredients:

- 8 lamb cutlets

- ½ cup mint leaves

- 6 garlic cloves

- 3 tbsp. lemon juice

- 1 tbsp. coriander seeds

- 4 tbsp. olive oil

- 1 tbsp. cumin, ground

- Zest of 2 lemons, grated

- A pinch of salt and black pepper

Directions:

1. In a blender, combine all the ingredients except the lamb and pulse well.

2. Rub the lamb cutlets with this mix, place them in your air fryer's basket and cook at 380°F for 15 minutes on each side. Serve with a side salad

Nutrition: Calories: 284; Fat: 13g; Fiber: 3g; Carbs: 5g; Protein: 15g

Adobo Beef

Preparation Time: 35 minutes Servings: 4

Ingredients:

• 1 lb. beef roast, trimmed

• 1 tbsp. olive oil

• . tsp. garlic powder

• . tsp. turmeric powder

• . tsp. oregano; dried

• A pinch of salt and black pepper

Directions:

1. Take a bowl and mix the roast with the rest of the ingredients and rub well.

2. Put the roast in the air fryer's basket and cook at 390°F for 30 minutes. Slice the roast, divide it between plates andserve with a side sala d.

Nutrition: Calories: 294; Fat: 12g; Fiber: 3g;

Carbs: 6g; Protein: 19g

Chipotle Pork Chops

Preparation Time: 40 minutes

Servings: 4

Ingredients:

- 4 pork chops, bone-in

- 2 ½ tbsp. ghee; melted

- ½ tsp. allspice

- 1 tsp. coconut sugar

- ½ tsp. garlic powder

- ½ tsp. chipotle chili powder

- ½ tsp. cinnamon powder

- A pinch of salt and black pepper

Directions:

1. Rub the pork chops with all the other ingredients, put them in your air fryer's basket and cook at 380°F for 35 minutes

2. Divide the chops between plates and serve with a side salad.

Nutrition: Calories: 287; Fat: 14g; Fiber: 4g; Carbs: 7g; Protein: 18g

EGGS AND DAIRY

Frittata with Porcini Mushrooms

Preparation Time: 40

minutes Servings: 4

Nutrition: 242 Calories; 16g Fat; 5.2g Carbs;

17.2g Protein; 2.8g Sugars; 1.3g Fiber

Ingredients

• 3 cups Porcini mushrooms, thinly sliced

• 1 tablespoon melted butter

• 1 shallot, peeled and slice into thin rounds

• 1 garlic cloves, peeled and finely minced

• 1 lemon grass, cut into 1-inch pieces

• 1/3 teaspoon table salt

• 8 eggs

• 1/2 teaspoon ground black pepper, preferably freshly ground

• 1 teaspoon cumin powder

• 1/3 teaspoon dried or fresh dill weed

• 1/2 cup goat cheese, crumbled

Directions

1. Melt the butter in a nonstick skillet that is placed over medium heat. Sauté the shallot, garlic, thinly sliced Porcini mushrooms, and lemon grass over am oderate heat until they have softened.Now, reserve the sautéed mixture.

2. Preheat your Air Fryer to 335 degrees F.Then, in a mixing bowl, beat the eggs until frothy. Now, add the seasoningsand mix to combine well.

3. Coat the sides and bottom of a baking dish with a thin layer of vegetable spray. Pour the egg/seasoning mixtureinto the baking dish; throw in the onion/mushroom sauté. Top with the crumbled goat cheese.

4. Place the baking dish in the Air Fryer cooking basket. Cook for about 32minutes or until your frittata is set.Enjoy!

VEGETABLES

Cream Cheese Mushroom Mix

Preparation time: 4 minutes

Cooking time: 20 minutes

Servings: 4

Ingredients:

- 1 pound brown mushrooms, halved

- 1 cup cream cheese, soft

- ¼ cup heavy cream

- 1 tablespoon rosemary, chopped

- 1 tablespoon olive oil

- 1 small yellow onion, chopped

- Salt and black pepper to the taste

Directions:

1. In your air fryer's pan, combine the mushrooms with the cream cheese and the other ingredients, toss and cook at 370 degrees F for 20 minutes.

2. Divide between plates and serve.

Nutrition: calories 202, fat 4, fiber 1, carbs 13, protein 4

Parmesan Artichokes and Tomatoes

Preparation time: 10 minutes

Cooking time: 15 minutes

Servings: 4

Ingredients:

- 2 cups canned artichoke hearts, drained
- and halved
- 1 cup parmesan, grated
- 2 tablespoons olive oil
- 1 cup cherry tomatoes, halved
- 3 garlic cloves, minced
- A pinch of salt and black pepper
- 1 tablespoon chives, chopped
- 1 teaspoon garlic powder

Directions:

1. In your air fryer, combine the artichoke hearts with the tomatoes and the other ingredients, toss gently and cook at 350 degrees F for 15 minutes.

2. Divide everything between plates and serve.

Nutrition: calories 200, fat 11, fiber 3, carbs 9, protein 4

Coconut Beets

Preparation time: 10 minutes

Cooking time: 25 minutes

Servings: 4

Ingredients:

- 4 beets, peeled and roughly cubed

- 1 cup coconut cream

- 1 tablespoon olive oil

- 2 garlic cloves, minced

- Juice of 1 lemon

- 1 tablespoon dill, chopped

Directions:

1. In your air fryer's pan, combine the beets with the cream and the other ingredients, toss and cook at 380 degrees F for 25 minutes.

2. Divide everything between plates and serve.

Nutrition: calories 213, fat 8, fiber 6, carbs 13, protein 6

Tomatoes and Kidney Beans

Preparation time: 10 minutes Cooking time: 20 minutes Servings: 4

Ingredients:

• 1 pound cherry tomatoes, halved

• 1 cup canned kidney beans, drained

• 2 tablespoons balsamic vinegar

• 2 tablespoons olive oil

• 3 garlic cloves, minced

• Salt and black pepper to the taste

• 1 tablespoon chives, chopped

Directions:

1. In your air fryer, combine the cherry tomatoes with the beans and the other ingredients, toss and cook at 380 degrees F for 20 minutes.

2. Divide between plates and serve.

Nutrition: calories 101, fat 3, fiber 3, carbs 4, protein 2

Oregano Kaloe

Preparation time: 10 minutes

Cooking time: 12 minutes

Servings: 4

Ingredients:

- 1 pound baby kale

- 2 tablespoons oregano, chopped

- 1 tablespoon olive oil

- 1 tablespoon feta cheese, crumbled

- A pinch of salt and black pepper

- 1 teaspoon cumin, ground

Directions:

1. In your air fryer, combine the kale with the oregano, oil and the other ingredients, toss and cook at 370 degrees F for 12 minutes.

2. Divide everything between plates and serve.

Nutrition: calories 140, fat 4, fiber 2, carbs 9, protein 5

SNACKS

Spinach Melts with Parsley Yogurt Dip

Preparation Time: 20 minutes

Servings: 4

Nutrition: 301 Calories; 25.2g Fat; 8.5g Carbs; 11.4g Protein; 2.2g Sugars; 3.7g Fiber

Ingredients

Spinach Melts:

- 2 cups spinach, torn into pieces

- 1 ½ cups cauliflower

- 1 tablespoon sesame oil

- 1/2 cup scallions, chopped

- 2 garlic cloves, minced

- 1/2 cup almond flour

- 1/4 cup coconut flour

- 1 teaspoon baking powder

- 1/2 teaspoon sea salt

- 1/2 teaspoon ground black pepper

- 1/4 teaspoon dried dill

- 1/2 teaspoon dried basil

- 1 cup cheddar cheese, shredded

Parsley Yogurt Dip:

- 1/2 cup Greek-Style yoghurt

- 2 tablespoons mayonnaise

- 2 tablespoons fresh parsley, chopped

- 1 tablespoon fresh lemon juice

- 1/2 teaspoon garlic, smashed

Directions

1. Place spinach in a mixing dish; pour in hot water. Drain and rinse well.

2. Add cauliflower to the steamer basket; steam until the cauliflower is tender about 5 minutes.

3. Mash the cauliflower; add the remaining ingredients for Spinach Melts and mix to combine well. Shape the mixture into patties and transfer them to the lightly greased cooking basket.

4. Bake at 330 degrees F for 14 minutes or until thoroughly heated.

5. Meanwhile, make your dipping sauce by whisking the remaining ingredients. Place in your refrigerator until ready to serve.

6. Serve the Spinach Melts with the chilled sauce on the side. Enjoy!

Indian Onion Rings, Bhaji

Preparation Time: 25 minutes

Servings: 4

Nutrition: 197 Calories; 17.2g Fat; 7.4g Carbs; 5g Protein; 2.5g Sugars; 3g Fiber

Ingredients

- 2 eggs, beaten

- 2 tablespoons olive oil

- 2 onions, sliced

- 1 green chili, deseeded and finely chopped

- 2 ounces almond flour

- 1 ounce coconut flour

- Salt and black pepper, to taste

- 1 teaspoon cumin seeds

- 1/2 teaspoon ground turmeric

Directions

1. Place all ingredients, except for the onions, in a mixing dish; mix to combine well, adding a little water to the mixture.

2. Once you've got a thick batter, add the onions; stir to coat well.

3. Cook in the preheated Air Fryer at 370 degrees F for 20 minutes flipping them halfway through the cooking time.

4. Work in batches and transfer to a serving platter. Enjoy!

Mozzarella, Brie and Artichoke Dip

Preparation Time: 22 minutes

Servings: 10

Nutrition: 128 Calories; 10.2g Fat; 2.7g Carbs; 7.3g Protein; 0.5g Sugars; 0.7g Fiber

Ingredients

- 2 cups arugula leaves, torn into pieces

- 1/3 can artichoke hearts, drained and chopped

- 1/2 cup Mozzarella cheese, shredded

- 1/3 cup sour cream

- 3 cloves garlic, minced

- 1/3 teaspoon dried basil

- 1 teaspoon sea salt

- 7 ounces Brie cheese

- 1/2 cup mayonnaise

- 1/3 teaspoon ground black pepper, or more to taste

- A pinch of ground allspice

Directions

1. Combine together the Brie cheese, mayonnaise, sour cream, garlic, basil, salt, ground black pepper, and the allspice.

2. Throw in the artichoke hearts and arugula; gently stir to combine. Transfer the prepared mixture to a baking dish. Now, scatter the Mozzarella cheese evenly over the top.

3. Bake in your Air Fryer at 325 degrees F for 17 minutes. Serve with keto veggie sticks. Bon appétit!

Picnic Chicken Nuggets

Preparation Time: 20 minutes

Servings: 6

Nutrition: 268 Calories; 18.9g Fat; 3.6g Carbs; 20.2g Protein; 1.2g Sugars; 0.9g Fiber

Ingredients

- 1 pound chicken breasts, slice into tenders

- 1/2 teaspoon cayenne pepper

- Salt and black pepper, to taste

- 1/4 cup almond meal

- 1 egg, whisked

- 1/2 cup parmesan cheese, freshly grated

- 1/4 cup mayo

- 1/4 cup barbecue sauce

Directions

1. Pat the chicken tenders dry with a kitchen towel. Season with the cayenne pepper, salt, and black pepper.

2. Dip the chicken tenders into the almond meal, followed by the egg. Press the chicken tenders into the parmesan cheese, coating evenly.

3. Place the chicken tenders in the lightly greased Air Fryer basket. Cook at 360 degrees for 9 to 12 minutes, turning them over to cook evenly.

4. In a mixing bowl, thoroughly combine the mayonnaise with the barbecue sauce. Serve the chicken nuggets with the sauce for dipping. Bon appétit!

Glazed Carrot Chips with Cheese

Preparation Time: 20 minutes

Servings: 3

Nutrition: 122 Calories; 10g Fat; 4.2g Carbs; 4.1g Protein; 0.4g Sugars; 0.6g Fiber

Ingredients

- 3 carrots, sliced into sticks

- 1 tablespoon coconut oil

- 1/3 cup Romano cheese, preferably freshly grated

- 2 teaspoons granulated garlic

- Sea salt and ground black pepper, to taste

Directions

1. Toss all ingredients in a mixing bowl until the carrots are coated on all sides.

2. Cook at 380 degrees F for 15 minutes, shaking the basket halfway through the cooking time.

3. Serve with your favorite dipping sauce. Bon appétit!

Kid-Friendly Cocktail Meatballs

Preparation Time: 20 minutes

Servings: 8

Nutrition: 350 Calories; 25.1g Fat; 1.2g Carbs; 28.3g Protein; 0.4g Sugars; 0.2g Fiber

Ingredients

- ½ teaspoon fine sea salt

- 1 cup Romano cheese, grated

- 3 cloves garlic, minced

- 1½ pound ground pork

- ½ cup scallions, finely chopped

- 2 eggs, well whisked

- 1/3 teaspoon cumin powder

- 2/3 teaspoon ground black pepper, or more to taste

- 2 teaspoons basil

Directions

1. Simply combine all the ingredients in a large-sized mixing bowl.

2. Shape into bite-sized balls; cook the meatballs in the air fryer for 18 minutes at 345 degrees F. Serve with some tangy sauce such as marinara sauce if desired. Bon appétit!

Twisted Wings with Blue Cheese

Preparation Time: 20 minutes

Servings: 6

Nutrition: 242 Calories; 12.1g Fat; 1.9g Carbs; 30g Protein; 0.7g Sugars; 0.2g Fiber

Ingredients

- 1 ½ pounds chicken wings

- 2 teaspoons sesame oil

- Kosher salt and ground black pepper, to taste

- 2 tablespoons tamari sauce

- 1 tablespoon rice vinegar

- 2 garlic cloves, minced

- 1 cup blue cheese, crumbled

Directions

1. Toss the chicken wings with the sesame oil, salt, and pepper. Add chicken wings to a lightly greased baking pan.

2. Roast the chicken wings in the preheated Air Fryer at 390 degrees F for 7 minutes. Turn them over once or twice to ensure even cooking.

3. In a mixing dish, thoroughly combine the tamari sauce, vinegar, garlic, and blue cheese.

4. Pour the sauce all over the chicken wings; bake an additional 5 minutes. Bon appétit!

Classic Kale Chips with Tahini

Preparation Time: 15 minutes

Servings: 4

Nutrition: 170 Calories; 15g Fat; 7.1g Carbs; 4.2g Protein; 0.7g Sugars; 2.7g Fiber

Ingredients

- 5 cups kale leaves, torn into 1-inch pieces

- 1 ½ tablespoons sesame oil

- 1/2 teaspoon shallot powder

- 1 teaspoon garlic powder

- 1/4 teaspoon porcini powder

- 1/2 teaspoon mustard seeds

- 1 teaspoon salt

- 1/3 cup tahini, sesame butter

- 1 tablespoon fresh lemon juice

- 2 cloves garlic, minced

Directions

1. Toss the kale with the sesame oil and seasonings.

2. Bake in the preheated Air Fryer at 350 degrees F for 10 minutes, shaking the cooking basket occasionally.

3. Bake until the edges are brown. Work in batches.

4. Meanwhile, make the sauce by whisking all ingredients in a small mixing bowl. Serve and enjoy!

Dad's Boozy Wings

Preparation Time: 1 hour 15 minutes

Servings: 4

Nutrition: 184 Calories; 9.6g Fat; 5.5g Carbs; 13.7g Protein; 3.5g Sugars; 0.5g Fiber

Ingredients

- 2 teaspoons coriander seeds

- 1 ½ tablespoons soy sauce

- 1/3 cup vermouth

- 3/4 pound chicken wings

- 1 ½ tablespoons each fish sauce

- 2 tablespoons melted butter

- 1 teaspoon seasoned salt

- Freshly ground black pepper, to taste

Directions

1. Rub the chicken wings with the black pepper and seasoned salt; now, add the other ingredients.

2. Next, soak the chicken wings in this mixture for 55 minutes in the refrigerator.

3. Air-fry the chicken wings at 365 degrees F for 16 minutes or until warmed through. Bon appétit!

DESSERT

Brownioes Muffins

Servings: 12

Preparation Time: 10 minutes

Cooking Time: 10 minutes

Ingredients

- 1 package Betty Crocker fudge brownie mix

- ¼ cup walnuts, chopped

- 1 egg

- 1/3 cup vegetable oil

- 2 teaspoons water

Instructions

1. In a bowl, mix well all the ingredients.

2. Set the temperature of air fryer to 300 degrees F. Grease 12 muffin molds.

3. Place mixture evenly into the prepared muffin molds.

4. Arrange the molds into an Air Fryer basket.

5. Air fry for 10 minutes or until a toothpick inserted in the center comes out clean.

6. Remove the muffin molds from air fryer and place onto a wire rack to cool for about 10 minutes.

7. Finally, invert the muffins onto wire rack to completely cool before serving.

Nutrition

Calories: 241

Carbohydrate: 36.9g

Protein: 2.8g

Fat: 9.6g

Sugar: 25g

Sodium: 155mg

Cheesecake Soufflé

Preparation Time: 15 minutes

Cooking time: 10 minutes

Servings: 2

Ingredients:

- 5 oz cream cheese

- 1 egg yolk

- 1 egg

- 1 teaspoon butter

- 2 tablespoons brown sugar

- ½ teaspoon vanilla extract

- ½ teaspoon almond flakes

Directions:

1. Beat the egg in the bowl.

2. Add the egg yolk and brown sugar.

3. Mix the mixture with the help of the hand mixer.

4. Then add butter, cream cheese, and vanilla extract.

5. Mix the mixture with the help of the hand mixer for 2 minutes at the maximum speed.

6. After this, pour the cream cheese mixture into 2 ramekins.

7. Preheat the air fryer to 350 F.

8. Place the ramekins in the air fryer basket and cook for 10 minutes.

9. The soufflé is cooked when you get the light brown color of the surface.

10. Let the soufflé chill for 5 minutes.

11. Then sprinkle the soufflé with the almond flakes.

12. Enjoy!

Nutrition: calories 363, fat 31.3, fiber 0.1, carbs 11.4, protein 9.6

Cherry Pie

Preparation Time: 15 minutes

Cooking time: 10 minutes

Servings: 2

Ingredients:

- 6 oz pie crust, uncooked

- 2 oz cherry, pitted

- 1 teaspoon brown sugar

- 1 teaspoon water

- ¼ teaspoon turmeric

Directions:

1. Roll the pie crust and place the cherries there.

2. Sprinkle the cherries with the brown sugar and turmeric.

3. Place the pie in the air fryer basket and sprinkle the edges of the pie with water.

4. Preheat the air fryer to 360 F.

5. Cook the pie for 10 minutes.

6. Then chill the cherry pie to the room temperature. Enjoy!

Nutrition: calories 157, fat 5, fiber 2.6, carbs 28, protein 2.6

Chocolate Profiteroles

Preparation Time: 15 minutes

Cooking time: 10 minutes

Servings: 2

Ingredients:

- 3 tablespoons flour

- 1 tablespoon butter

- 1 egg

- 2 tablespoon water

- 2 tablespoon whipped cream

Directions:

1. Boil the water and melt the butter.

2. Combine together boiled water, butter, and flour.

3. Mix the mixture and beat the egg.

4. Then mix the dough with the help of the mixer.

5. When you get the plastic dough – transfer it to the pastry bag.

6. Preheat the air fryer to 360 F.

7. Make the profiteroles with the help of the special nozzle and transfer them in the air fryer basket.

8. Cook the profiteroles for 10 minutes,

9. Then chill the profiteroles and cut them crosswise.

10. Fill the profiteroles with the whipped cream.

11. Enjoy!

Nutrition: calories 338, fat 25.4, fiber 0.6, carbs 19.1, protein 8 .7

Oats Cookies

Preparation Time: 10 minutes

Cooking time: 9 minutes

Servings: 2

Ingredients:

- 3 tablespoon oatmeal flour

- 2 tablespoon sour cream

- 1 tablespoon brown sugar

- 1 teaspoon butter

- 1 pinch salt

- ½ teaspoon ground cardamom

- 1 egg

Directions:

1. Beat the egg in the bowl and whisk it.

2. Add the oatmeal flour and flour in the whisked egg.

3. After this, add sour cream, brown sugar, butter, salt, and ground cardamom.

4. Mix the mixture to get the homogenous dough.

5. Preheat the air fryer to 360 F.

6. Cover the air fryer basket with the parchment.

7. Make the medium cookies from the dough. Use the spoon for this step.

8. Place the cookies in the air fryer basket and cook for 9 minutes.

9. When the cookies are cooked – chill them well.

10. Taste and enjoy!

Nutrition: calories 115, fat 7, fiber 0.8, carbs 9.3, protein 4.2

Stuffed Baked Apples

Preparation Time: 3 minutes • Cooking Time: 12 minutes • Servings: 4

INGREDIENTS

- 4tbsps. honey
- ¼ cup brown sugar
- ½ cup raisins
- ½ cup crushed walnuts
- 4large apples

DIRECTIONS:

1. Preheat Air Fryer to a temperature of 350°F (180°C).
2. Cut the apples from the stem and remove the inner using spoon.
3. Now fill each apple with raisins, walnuts, honey, and brown sugar.
4. Transfer apples in a pan and place in Air Fryer basket, cook for 12 minutes.
5. Serve.

NUTRITION: Calories: 324 Protein: 2.8 g Fat: 6.99 g Carbs: 70.31 g

Chocolate Yoogurt Muffins

Servings: 9

Preparation Time: 15 minutes

Cooking Time: 10 minutes

Ingredients

- 1½ cups all-purpose flour

- ¼ cup sugar

- 2 teaspoons baking powder

- ½ teaspoon salt

- 1 cup yogurt

- 1/3 cup vegetable oil

- 1 egg

- 2 teaspoons vanilla extract

- ¼ cup mini chocolate chips

- ¼ cup pecans, chopped

Instructions

1. In a bowl, mix well flour, sugar, baking powder, and salt.

2. In another bowl, add the yogurt, oil, egg, and vanilla extract and whisk until well combined.

3. Add the flour mixture and mix until just combined.

4. Fold in the chocolate chips and pecans.

5. Set the temperature of air fryer to 355 degrees F. Grease 9 muffin molds.

6. Place mixture evenly into the prepared muffin molds.

7. Arrange the muffin molds into an air fryer basket.

8. Air fry for 10 minutes or until a toothpick inserted in the center comes out clean.

9. Remove the muffin molds from air fryer and place onto a wire rack to cool for about 10 minutes.

10. Finally, invert the muffins onto wire rack to completely cool before serving.

Nutrition

Calories: 246

Carbohydrate: 27.3g

Protein: 5g

Fat: 12.9g

Sugar: 10.2g

Sodium: 159mg

Cherry Pie

Preparation Time: 15 minutes

Cooking time: 10 minutes

Servings: 2

Ingredients:

- 6 oz pie crust, uncooked

- 2 oz cherry, pitted

- 1 teaspoon brown sugar

- 1 teaspoon water

- ¼ teaspoon turmeric

Directions:

1. Roll the pie crust and place the cherries there.

2. Sprinkle the cherries with the brown sugar and turmeric.

3. Place the pie in the air fryer basket and sprinkle the edges of the pie with water.

4. Preheat the air fryer to 360 F.

5. Cook the pie for 10 minutes.

6. Then chill the cherry pie to the room temperature.

7. Enjoy!

Nutrition: calories 157, fat 5, fiber 2.6, carbs 28, protein 2.6

Brownies Muffins

Servings: 12

Preparation Time: 10 minutes

Cooking Time: 10 minutes

Ingredients

- 1 package Betty Crocker fudge brownie mix

- ¼ cup walnuts, chopped

- 1 egg

- 1/3 cup vegetable oil

- 2 teaspoons water

Instructions

1. In a bowl, mix well all the ingredients.

2. Set the temperature of air fryer to 300 degrees F. Grease 12 muffin molds.

3. Place mixture evenly into the prepared muffin molds.

4. Arrange the molds into an Air Fryer basket.

5. Air fry for 10 minutes or until a toothpick inserted in the center comes out clean.

6. Remove the muffin molds from air fryer and place onto a wire rack to cool for about 10 minutes.

7. Finally, invert the muffins onto wire rack to completely cool before serving.

Nutrition

Calories: 241

Carbohydrate: 36.9g

Protein: 2.8g

Fat: 9.6g

Sugar: 25g

Sodium: 155mg

Cheesecake Soufflé

Preparation Time: 15 minutes

Cooking time: 10 minutes

Servings: 2

Ingredients:

- 5 oz cream cheese

- 1 egg yolk

- 1 egg

- 1 teaspoon butter

- 2 tablespoons brown sugar

- ½ teaspoon vanilla extract

- ½ teaspoon almond flakes

Directions:

1. Beat the egg in the bowl.

2. Add the egg yolk and brown sugar.

3. Mix the mixture with the help of the hand mixer.

4. Then add butter, cream cheese, and vanilla extract.

5. Mix the mixture with the help of the hand mixer for 2 minutes at the maximum speed.

6. After this, pour the cream cheese mixture into 2 ramekins.

7. Preheat the air fryer to 350 F.

8. Place the ramekins in the air fryer basket and cook for 10 minutes.

9. The soufflé is cooked when you get the light brown color of the surface.

10. Let the soufflé chill for 5 minutes.

11. Then sprinkle the soufflé with the almond flakes.

12. Enjoy!

Nutrition: calories 363, fat 31.3, fiber 0.1, carbs 11.4, protein 9.6

Chocolate Yogurt Muffins

Servings: 9

Preparation Time: 15 minutes

Cooking Time: 10 minutes

Ingredients

- 1½ cups all-purpose flour

- ¼ cup sugar

- 2 teaspoons baking powder

- ½ teaspoon salt

- 1 cup yogurt

- 1/3 cup vegetable oil

- 1 egg

- 2 teaspoons vanilla extract

- ¼ cup mini chocolate chips

- ¼ cup pecans, chopped

Instructions

1. In a bowl, mix well flour, sugar, baking powder, and salt.

2. In another bowl, add the yogurt, oil, egg, and vanilla extract and whisk until well combined.

3. Add the flour mixture and mix until just combined.

4. Fold in the chocolate chips and pecans.

5. Set the temperature of air fryer to 355 degrees F. Grease 9 muffin molds.

6. Place mixture evenly into the prepared muffin molds.

7. Arrange the muffin molds into an air fryer basket.

8. Air fry for 10 minutes or until a toothpick inserted in the center comes out clean.

9. Remove the muffin molds from air fryer and place onto a wire rack to cool for about 10 minutes.

10. Finally, invert the muffins onto wire rack to completely cool before serving.

Nutrition

Calories: 246

Carbohydrate: 27.3g

Protein: 5g

Fat: 12.9g

Sugar: 10.2g

Sodium: 159mg

Chocolate Profiteroles

Preparation Time: 15 minutes

Cooking time: 10 minutes

Servings: 2

Ingredients:

- 3 tablespoons flour

- 1 tablespoon butter

- 1 egg

- 2 tablespoon water

- 2 tablespoon whipped cream

Directions:

1. Boil the water and melt the butter.

2. Combine together boiled water, butter, and flour.

3. Mix the mixture and beat the egg.

4. Then mix the dough with the help of the mixer.

5. When you get the plastic dough – transfer it to the pastry bag.

6. Preheat the air fryer to 360 F.

7. Make the profiteroles with the help of the special nozzle and transfer them in the air fryer basket.

8. Cook the profiteroles for 10 minutes,

9. Then chill the profiteroles and cut them crosswise.

10. Fill the profiteroles with the whipped cream.

11. Enjoy!

Nutrition: calories 338, fat 25.4, fiber 0.6, carbs 19.1, protein 8 .7

Oats Cookies

Preparation Time: 10 minutes

Cooking time: 9 minutes

Servings: 2

Ingredients:

- 3 tablespoon oatmeal flour

- 2 tablespoon sour cream

- 1 tablespoon brown sugar

- 1 teaspoon butter

- 1 pinch salt

- ½ teaspoon ground cardamom

- 1 egg

Directions:

1. Beat the egg in the bowl and whisk it.

2. Add the oatmeal flour and flour in the whisked egg.

3. After this, add sour cream, brown sugar, butter, salt, and ground cardamom.

4. Mix the mixture to get the homogenous dough.

5. Preheat the air fryer to 360 F.

6. Cover the air fryer basket with the parchment.

7. Make the medium cookies from the dough. Use the spoon for this step.

8. Place the cookies in the air fryer basket and cook for 9 minutes.

9. When the cookies are cooked – chill them well.

10. Taste and enjoy!

Nutrition: calories 115, fat 7, fiber 0.8, carbs 9.3, protein 4.2

Roasted Pineapples with Vanilla Zest

Preparation Time: 5 minutes • Cooking Time: 8 minutes • Servings: 4

INGREDIENTS

- 2anise stars
- ¼ cup orange juice
- 1tsp. lime juice
- 1vanilla pod
- 2tbsps. caster sugar
- ¼ cup pineapple juice
- 1lb. pineapple slices

DIRECTIONS

1. Preheat Air Fryer to a temperature of 350°F (180°C).
2. Take a baking pan that can fit into Air Fryer basket.
3. Now add pineapple juice, sugar, orange juice, anise stars, and vanilla pod into a pan and mix well.
4. Place in pineapple slices evenly and transfer pan into Air Fryer basket.
5. Cook for 8 minutes.
6. Serve!

NUTRITION: Calories: 90 Protein: 0.79 g Fat: 1.17 g Carbs: 23.22 g

Vanilla Coconut Pie

Preparation Time: 15 minutes • Cooking Time: 12 minutes • Servings: 4

INGREDIENTS

- Shredded coconut, 1 cup
- Granulated monk fruit, ½ cup
- Vanilla extract, 1 ½ tsps.
- Eggs,
- Almond milk, 1 ½ cup
- Coconut flour, ½ cup
- Butter, ¼ cup

DIRECTIONS

1. Combine all the ingredients in a suitable mixing bowl using a wooden spatula to form a batter.
2. Pour this batter into a 6-inch pie pan then place this pan in the air fryer basket.
3. Return the basket to the air fryer then cook the pie for 12 minutes at 3700 F on Air Fry Mode.
4. Allow it to cool then serve.

NUTRITION: Calories: 272   Fat: 27 g   Carbs: 7.8 g
Protein: 5.3 g

Cookie Dough Ball

Preparation Time: 15 minutes • Cooking Time: 5 minutes • Servings: 4

INGREDIENTS:

- Vanilla extract, ½ tsp.
- Swerve sugar substitute, 1 tbsp.
- Egg,
- Mini sugar-free chocolate chips, 3 tbsps.
- Coconut flour, ½ cup
- Xanthan gum, ¼ tsp.
- Coconut oil.
- Baking powder, ½ tsp.
- Almond flour, ½ cup
- Trivia sugar substitute, ½ tbsp.
- Melted butter, ½ tbsp.
- Cinnamon, ¼ tsp.

DIRECTIONS

1. In a mixing bowl, incorporate all the ingredients.
2. Whisk in egg, vanilla, and melted butter.
3. Mix well until a smooth dough forms then fold in chocolate chips.
4. Roll the dough into a ball then refrigerate until air fryer is ready.

5. Grease the air fryer basket with coconut oil and preheat the fryer to 375 degrees F.

6. Divide the dough into cookie-sized balls and place them in the basket.

7. Set the basket back to the air fryer and cook them for 5 minutes on Air Fry Mode.

8. Serve.

NUTRITION: Calories: 179   Fat: 10.7 g   Carbs: 24.2 g   Protein: 6.9 g

Conclusion

Thanks for getting to the end of **Simply Air Fryer Cookbook 2021: The Essential Guide To Cooking Affordable, Easy and Delicious Air Fryer Crisp Recipes for Everyone**, we hope it was informative and able to provide you with all the tools you need to achieve your goals, whatever they may be.

The air fryer can take some time to get used to. It takes time to determine new habits and become familiar with food replacement methods, including how to make cheap food tasty and satisfying.

But if you keep up, it can become a replacement lifestyle that is natural and convenient. It can also lead to some major health improvements, especially if you suffer from any condition, the keto diet proves helpful. And better health can mean fewer doctor visits and lower medical bills.

Finally, if you found this book helpful in any way, a review is always appreciated!

CPSIA information can be obtained
at www.ICGtesting.com
Printed in the USA
BVHW050849120421
604725BV00004B/173

9 781801 941150